whiskey & fox | vol. 4 no. 1 | march 2010

I0449930

whiskey & fox

doing politics with an-imals

Whiskey & Fox

Pittsburgh & Madison & Brooklyn

2010

editorial collective:

Daniel C. Remein, *founding editor*

Sarah Bagley, *'theory' editor*

Sten Carlson, *'poetry' editor*

Blaire Zeiders, *historiographical editor*

Whiskey & Fox is a journal of poetry, theory, and queer-heterotopoi. Please send all correspondance other than submissons, including queries concerning where to send books for review, to **editors@whiskeyandfox.org**. *Whiskey & Fox* does not always accept unsoclited submissions. For information on calls for open submissions, please reference **whiskey&fox.org**.

this issue is typeset, in roman and italic,
Monotype Joanna & **Helvetica Neue**

doing politics with animals

Doing Politics with Animals is not to be taken as a topic, nor as theme, but rather as a title, or a name. That such a title would open this new phase in the life of this little journal we hope carries a certain force: a promise/threat commensurate with Giorgio Agamben's hope that "Perhaps there is still a way in which living beings can sit at the messianic banquet of the righteous without taking on a historical task [such as, *pace* Heidegger, academically sanctioned national socialism] and without setting the anthropological machine into action"[1]; or, alternately, and negatively put, we would suggest that to "render inoperative the machine that governs our conception of man will therefore mean no longer to seek new—more effective or more authentic—articulations, but rather to show the central emptiness, the hiatus that—within man—separates man and animal."[2]

But the suggestion that this issue might *open* a new phase in the life of this journal highlights a privilege generally accorded only to beings which get distinguished as human—as not-animal. We follow Agamben's critique of Heidegger. For Heidegger, the animal may get to be in the open, but it is not considered to experience the open as open, in relation to something concealed. The human will be distinguishable as what can experience this open as open, in relation to a non-open. This path of articulating the human in the supposed space of its difference from the animal leaves the human only intelligible by positing animal existence as this "exposure without disconcealement";[3] and it leads to a violence enacted upon the animal: "Perhaps it is not the case that being and the human world have been pre-supposed in order to reach the animal by means of subtraction...perhaps the contrary is also, and even more, true, that is, that the openness of the human world (insofar as it is also and primarily an openness to the essential conflict between disconcealment and concealment) can be achieved only by means of an operation enacted upon the not-open of the animal world."[4] Our experience of possibility is predicated on a conception of the animal which requires such an operation on the animal world: where Being can be defined to such an extent as *human* being only by a violent procedure of keeping the animal within *our* being. Or, as this volume's respondent Karl Steel has put it, at least since the Middle Ages, "animals *must* suffer to guarantee that only humans can reason, speak, and finally be received into immortality....no one's humanity is reassured by destroying a rock."[5] All too often we find "the foundation of the human subject on a humiliated animal object."[6] For, the animal cannot be animal if it can only *be* in the mode of being-dominated/humiliated, being where we demand it so that we can keep the difference between human and animal as the (empty) center of being-human. For Agamben, since the animal "is outside of being...outside in an exteriority more external than any open," then "to let the animal be would then mean: to let it be *outside of being.*[7]"

A possible best hope: the promise-threats of queer poetics, a sniffing out of the grasping arms of the human and gently, but forebodingly, placing toothèd jaws around them; words that lick the bottoms of the human without letting on whether they will be tongues or flames. For, even if we remain unsatisfied with the above formulations of the human, we would not give up on the human; we remain committed to it, even if that commitment takes shape in the form of this generous threat of animal jaws which frame our scenting and licking of the human and its self-formings in history. To let the animal be outside being? To *do something alongside it* rather than to be with it? To leave our own ontology behind? Not to do animal politics or human politics, but to do politics as a way of being (human), rather than demanding a humiliating form of being?

This issue which is titled and not themed with the words "Doing Politics with Animals" would still open something, and it would still be a new phase in the life of the journal. But what kind of life and from what perspective? What would be the life of any journal? We submit it lies not in what it is, in its ontology, but in its operation, perhaps its *hauntology* or what might be its *animality*: that it might expose readers to a no-openable open: poems that do not mean, words that are never read, motives not uncovered because operating and not being. That we may seem a little late on the question of the animal, that it is already perhaps a mainstreamed and popular mode of academic discourse, that even the *PMLA*[8] has already taken it up as an object of knowledge for one of its issues, does not perturb us. This does not concern us becaue we would hope that, in a certain sense, *Whiskey & Fox* is not. This beast would do, not be. And the figure for what it opens, the figure of this differently operating phase of life: the jaws of whatever would lovingly gnaw away at the human life of a journal, would nurse the young of the life of a journal from the perspective of its animal, bestial life. Can a journal be outside of being and let-be outside of being? Can it *operate* or *do*? If the human will have such a hard time doing anything non-violent with animals, might that most inhuman of tekné's, language, do the trick? What can a journal do with animals? A journal that, seen from the perspective of life exposed at the threshold of the always-open (as the so-open-it-might-as-well-be-closed), only opens wider.

The Editors, Pittsburgh & Madison & Brooklyn, Fall 2009

notes

[1] Giorgio Agamben, *The Open: Man and Animal*, trans. Kevin Attell (Stanford: Stanford Univeristy Press, 2004), 92.   [2] ibid.   [3] ibid., 62.   [4] ibid.   [5] Karl Steel, "How to Make a Human," *Exemplaria* 20:1 (2008), 3-27, (19).   [6] ibid., 18.   [7] Agamben, 91.   [8] See PMLA 124: 2 (Jan 2009).

Whiskey & Fox

I could pull this, right, and the veins
Would uncoil on a doll's head ribbons
Look like, marionetteer
There's a silent radio in my feed
Tube, rivers, keep coming next dream through
The teeth I could feed myself, a spiritual
Exercise in gender and number zero stands
For deserter's head on a mast, if
One of you could please tell me my skin is
Like falling from the sun streaked sky
Off a despot's thumb, my body could drop
Backwards in a tub of scalded cat's
Milk, headless, head on

Robin Clarke

White Hose

A welcome adage
treated with relief. Summer
closets taken apart during
continuity breaks.
The rumors, for once, are

true. One coast left
to its devices. All I did
was twiddle the knobs.

The lamp is off. You
like it that way. Fish
tender, greens slightly bitter. The
wine is red. Television
finishes our sentences.

All this and the weekend isn't over.
If you had other names, I would use them.

Jeff T. Johnson

Bull Dragged from Arena

which we only barely noticed
for the torreador's gilded strut
beneath the stadium's swoon, hat
in hand, the occasional rose twisting
through the air to his feet, dragged
limp and drooling by horses
adorned with ribbons
and bells.

Ross Gay

Peripatetic Landscape

The map becomes a landscape
that disappears

                            Here
regenerates in real time

As one expatiates the new
                      location

Kicking through scraps
in relief   A body

           to replace
Orientation

Jeff T. Johnson

Better Habit

Get to the good part. Densely

                        We fool

You: a massacre waning

To discomfit the alarms

Which were so neatly situated

Above doors, the building

                        To themselves

Just so   The better part

Of the day   overcome by shade

In the new hemisphere

We will know our places   A

Backyard fantasy with legs

Tell your associates   we know what

We are doing   In the glow erupting

From appropriated icons

It is our job to get along   It is

Our job to find a way out

Jeff T. Johnson

Speech Act

We are who we think
others think we are
is Joshua's definition of sociology
though he pawns it off on everyone

By upsetting
expectations, he allows us
to absorb his odd and fleeting
truths about love and hate
and beauty and regret
and all the things that a society
institutionalized on greed and
power pours into us

A few key phrases escaped
during a spell of laughter

A light rain, or a brief one

Drums rush past
the alleyway
where we left you
eyes cocked to the side

If only you had a hat to match
that jacket of fog

Oh, but it meant nothing
please forget me
I assure you

This was years ago, before the curse

Jeff T. Johnson

Naming the Kingdom

300 years ago, Swedish botanist, Carl Linnaeus set out to name all plants and animals

with a simple two unit Latin taxonomy that identified genus and species only.

From the cacophony of competing nomenclatures, he wrote a simple, memorable system.

God Created, but Linnaeus Organized, they said in extravagant praise of him.

The Linnaean names became so accepted that the 1735 frontispiece of Systema naturae

even shows God in the Garden of Eden using the Linnaean system to name new plants.

And Linnaeus was a great promoter of his own idea.

For 20 years he conducted public expeditions to locate new plants and animals.

They were organized like a military campaign.

As many as three hundred people were sub-divided into cohorts.

Some were note takers, some bird shooters, some specimen collectors.

The fields were broken into districts and Linnaeus' army scoured them thoroughly.

The rector of Uppsala University called it a rude inquisition of the pastures.

Each time a new specimen was discovered a bugle sounded to spur on the troops.

After up to 12 hours, a parade of proto-botanists merrily unfurled its banner

and the throng blocked the highways singing and marching in pure joy.

Gary Lehmann

Get Money

Able to fly, he buys her sequined leotards. If she could
get money, they might live together.
He felt a sense of shame
telling her a lie. She felt shame
giving him away. He bought a glass of water and $10,000.
She pulled hands out of the garden; an outburst of
color became her dominant emotion.
He, quite simply, had to be taught, was
furious. The ligaments of her
spine form a fish's fin. To whom does he owe this
defamation of character? She's a real
species, a letter or number too
bound in cloth, cut so as to fix
teaching responsibility. He must produce
more books than box, abundant
melon in lieu of torn clothing, then
rot and decay.
She isn't able to understand the way
education moves through the house, causing calcified tissue
to deteriorate, rotting the whole tooth.
He sighs, spreading fingers.

Claire Donato

Manifest

You have not heard
the punctuation
and the fury

I was about to be your army
but we slept and

now we hear something outside
wet sky in our haircuts
soft ululations on the driveway

This is what we said when you were gone

Jeff T. Johnson

"And now for the feather boa sequence."

Any true contradiction reflects the nature of forgetting. That is, one's fantasy of insulting one's way to the top is diminished by the fact that one is wearing a fedora.

To believe that something exists is linked to contradiction; one must begin with a bouquet of flowers. Leave them on the banister near the entrance to our house. *Be careful when you lock yourself indoors.*

Meanwhile, the candy cane sale was a smashing success. All sixty 8th graders purchased canes for their friends and teachers. Special thanks to the class representatives from grade 7 for distributing the treats.

… but what about Jimmy, who did not receive a cane? He sent a flurry but received nothing in return. Is it possible his friends are all fruitions? At the bottom of the stairs, he is stretching out his hamstring, pulling a muscle. Now his triceps are pulled up against his neck. He is tempted to send feedback. He practices revision. The chart was a gift from the man with a conservative expression who threatened to climb the stairs.

And now, Jimmy, age 22, sits anxiously in the audience, waits for something to happen.

Claire Donato

Selections from **The Excavation of Light at the Wedding**

Do you have any actual memories of being in the room?

> They learned quickly enough that their hands could
> be confused with the flickering of lights or the swel
>
> ————————————————————————
>
> you know that i haven't said i i haven't wanted to reveal

How did you find the answer so easily?

> It is a process of elimination. It can only be described
> in terms of what it is not. Neither a machine nor a pers
>
> ————————————————————————
>
> tracing the bodies top to bottom i learned how to spot a lo

Can we go off the record for a minute?

The safest place is between the back of the couch and the cushion. There is nothing that can touch you said

we should always behave as though extinction were inev

Were you there when the sound stopped altogether?

When movies become suspenseful sometimes they cut out the soundtrack. Someone was singing the Ave Ma

when i saw the blood the ocean swelled the climax was a l

Rebecca Mertz

"Falling Out of Language, Animally"

I am a worm, and not a man—**Psalm 22.6**
Animals praise you, by the mouth of those who consider them—**Augustine**
Being does not see itself. Perhaps it listens to itself.—**Gaston Bachelard**

So let me begin by hearing one voice speak to another. "A moment arrives," says Jean-Luc Nancy, "when one can no longer feel anything but anger, an absolute anger, against so many discourses, so many texts, that have no other care than to make a little more sense, to redo or perfect delicate works of signification."[1] "But," says Tristram Shandy, "with an ass, I can commune forever."[2] We have had (and are again having) enough of words. Perhaps speaking to animals, or at least to the animal, may help.

More precisely, I overhear in this miniature found dialogue the following premises and possibilities:

1. That we have language only insofar as we belong to it and that our belonging to language depends in a fundamental way on our belonging to, our being through and with the animal. Heidegger says, "language is the house of being."[3] Lao Tzu says, "We make doors and windows for a room; / But it is these empty spaces that make the room livable."[4] Our language-house needs openings, through which animals may sometimes enter, out of which we may sometimes fall. The openings are the spaces of intersection between our relationship to language and our relationship to the animal. Through them we do the remembering that preserves at once language and animal from the violence of reification. "Evil," says Agamben, "is the forgetting of the transcendence inherent in the very taking-place of things." Dwelling in language this way, inhering to its own and its object's taking place, has to do with cultivating the experience that being before the animal demands, with taking seriously the inner movement

22

to *consider* the animal, literally, to be with it the way one is with the stars, in wonder. This means practicing language that on the one hand returns meaning to the actuality of things and bodies, and on the other returns language to ourselves, to our being, to what is not thing or body. Such language recognizes, sees the animal in a double sense. It speaks of things, bodies as they are, in their actuality, which means seeing everything as animated by its being, as animal. And it speaks *from* ourselves as we are, which means seeing our own prediscursive or animal being, what Husserl calls "that as yet dumb experience . . . which we are concerned to lead to the pure expression of its own meaning." Seeing thus might be called *speaking animally*, as both articulating everything as a form of life (existence as animation) and articulating as the animal "would," naively, as it were, speaking what presents itself before our words for it, so that the word does not blind. Speaking thus, the human enacts its "higher" animality, its having of language as the faculty which produces is ownmost perception, the ever-opening articulation of self and world which we gaze upon in animal life as the spectacle of our own possibility. "See or perish," says Teilhard de Chardin, "this is the situation imposed on every element of the universe by the mysterious gift of existence. And thus, to a higher degree, this is the human condition." To be at home in our language, in the world, means using it to see, to live. So speaking animally, as I have sketched it, is essentially deictic, in the way that Merleau-Ponty defines the end, and limit, of philosophy: "Our relationship to the world, as it is untiringly enunciated within us, is not a thing which can be any further clarified by analysis; philosophy can only place it once more before our eyes and present it for our ratification."

  2. That language is the we, a community to which animal, human, and all we see belongs. In other words, the ground of language, its very possibility, is the *unity of life*. This unity is not something transcendent or outside the world, but rather constitutes the world as such, that is, it is of a

piece with the plural fact of our being here in the first place, our topos. Language thus belongs to the originary goodness of world, to the goodness of its taking place. So I read the hexameral creation formula—God said ... and saw that it was good—as signifying goodness not as a worldly property but *as the very opening whereby the said becomes the seen*. Compare Giorgio Agamben's comment on the event of beings: "God or the good or the place does not take place, but is the taking-place of the entities, their innermost exteriority. The being-worm of the worm, the being-stone of the stone, is divine. That the world is, that something can appear and have a face, that there is exteriority and non-latency as the determination and the limit of every thing: this is the good." Language, like being, is not a thing, but a belonging, a participation in the innermost exteriority of the world's taking place.

3. That language, as the wall or structuring principle of this community, neither simply surrounds nor separates human and animal, but rather separates by surrounding and surrounds by separating them, and so creates the distinction *between*, us. This betweeness of language, which Derrida deals with as the *animot* and according to which the human appears (from Adam's naming of the animals to the Fischer-Price See N Say toy) as the animal-naming animal, is only one instance of the more general subject-object structure whereby every individuated being is a/the world-event. In other words, the idea that language is the animal/human boundary is simply the speciesization, our speciesization, of an omnipresent boundary that has a linguistic structure. For a picture of this structure, I turn to Samuel Beckett's The Unnamable as a possible model monologue of every being: "Perhaps that's what I am, the thing that divides the world in two, on the one side the outside, on the other side the inside, that can be as thin as foil, I'm neither one side nor the other, I'm in the middle, I'm the partition, I've two surfaces and no thickness, perhaps that's what I feel, myself vibrating, I'm the tympanum, on the one hand the mind, on the other the world, I don't belong

to either." Moreover, these lines also dramatize speaking as self-listening. So all entities, my intuition insists, are to be included in this truth, in the phenomenon whereby the self (animal, human, whatever) is an event centered on an inner place where speaking and hearing are indistinguishable. Every *there* is a *here*. All entities *hear* themselves. Some beings *speak* their self-listening more and more intentionally than others. Indeed, this difference may well be greater *within* the human species than between animal and human.

4. That a purely human discourse, a language for us by us in the narrow sense, is intolerable, maybe impossible, a dark, suffocating house of being. Such language, for which Nancy's anger towards the asymptotic "little more sense" of critical discourse provides a clear image, is a language that merely means, language reducing itself, and its object along with it, to a thing, a self-enclosure, meaning-products, and this constitutes a forgetting or denial of the other dimension of language which has to do with its belonging to being, language's operation within what Gumbrecht calls "the production of presence," the deictic and auto-deictic, or pointing and self-pointing, procedures through which things reemerge and are recognized as beings. In other words, intolerably human discourse is language in denial of being's discursivity, in the restriction of what it is to what it means, against which we may set Bachelard's account of the human as "half-open being," as something structured by the fact that "language bears within itself the dialectics of open and closed. Through *meaning* it encloses, while through poetic expression, it opens up." Or, we can say that the two "halves" of human being as half-open are poetry and philosophy, and that it is through the separation or enclosure of one from the other that language becomes a place where *we*, our being, is not at home. Agamben terms such separation "the scission of the word" and identifies it as essential to Western culture and the birth of criticism: "the scission of the word is construed to mean that poetry possesses its object without knowing it

while philosophy knows its object without possessing it. . . . In our culture knowledge . . . is divided between inspired-ecstatic and rational-conscious poles, neither ever succeeding in wholly reducing the other . . . What is thus overlooked is the fact that every authentic poetic project is directed toward knowledge, just has every authentic act of philosophy is always directed toward joy. . . . Criticism is born at the moment when the scission reaches its extreme point. It is situated where, in Western culture, the word comes unglued from itself . . . and can be expressed in the formula according to which it neither represents nor knows, but knows the representation." This of course suggests an *inherent* principle or cause within philosophical and critical engagement with the animal, namely, that the animal fascinates these discourses precisely as "living art," representation that cannot be understood as representation, unrepresentable representation, i.e. real, present being. In a world without animal presence, what would we *say*? Georges-Louis Buffon, the 18th-century French natural scientist, said "If animals did not exist, the nature of man would be even more incomprehensible." So I imagine that if animals did not exist—an embarrassingly ridiculous hypothetical—this incomprehensibility would threaten language itself, would cause humans to forget, refuse, or in some other way lose the ability, to speak. Companion piece to *Children of Men*?

What does it mean, then, to fall out of language with animals? My desire to discover a meaning for this phrase began with recognizing it as an absent term of Agamben's description of animal/human language boundary: "Animals do not enter language, they are already inside it. Man, instead, by having an infancy, by preceding speech, splits this single language and, in order to speak, has to constitute himself as the subject of language—he has to say I. . . . Contrary to ancient traditional beliefs, from this point of view man is not the 'animal possessing language', but instead the animal deprived of language and obliged, therefore, to receive it from outside himself." If it is entering language that makes one, like birth, generically human, might it not be that exiting language, as a mastering of this entry, as knowing how to climb back out, has something to do with being, despite the poverty of the term, fully human? Is falling out of language, or letting language fall from us, or throwing language over itself, something that fulfills the hope of the human, its transcendent/perverse desire to be more than animal? And yet this fall, as the fall of a being that has language, can only happen through language. In the hearing of language's silence? In its speaking of the unsaid? This is the point in my talk, at the end, where it would be normal to start talking about silence as a plenitude rather than absence of language and to conclude with a poetic description of the beautiful, awkward silences we sometimes share with animals, our philosophical familiars. Instead I will deliver something more concrete, a detail from one of the most remembered examples of animal-human communion, in which it is discovered that even nothing can speak: "Since he had now been made simple by grace and not by nature, he began to accuse himself of negligence for not having preached to the birds before, since they listened to the word of God with such reverence. And thus it came about that, from that day on, he exhorted all birds, all animals, all reptiles, and even nonexistent creatures to praise and love the creator."

notes

1   The Birth to Presence, trans. Brian Holmes (Stanford: Stanford University Press, 1993), 5.

2   Laurence Sterne, The Life and Opinions of Tristram Shandy, Gentleman (New York: Penguin, 2003), VII.32, p. 471.

3   Martin Heidegger, "Letter on 'Humanism," trans. Frank A. Capuzzi, in Pathmarks, ed. William McNeill (Cambridge: Cambridge University Press, 1998), 239.

4   The Tao Ching, trans. John C.H. Wu (Boston: Shambala, 1989), ch. 11, p. 23.

Nicola Masciandaro

Again the red ball springs the dynamo
Trumps the wooden leg, Trojan
Horse blue sky dream of blue
Pulled from the eye and pinned, as if
A wild boar breathed down
The vegetation and stirs
Vegetation precisely on the verge
Of anything left to do but scrying?
Whispering and scrying
The ground for, blood
Piss or white sex, boys' singing
Balls or razed sky cut on a perfect
Diagonal gash, swallowed by mouth
Spoke thus the name

Robin Clarke

In Cook Forest she walks eleven miles through the virgin oak trees down the steep path toward the creek running *Saltwater,* *saltwater.*

She walks down the cavernous mountain toward the creek streaming below the forest's path. As a girl, she sat in place of monstrous, hovering trees; thunderstorms dispensed little comfort; one flooded the creek, spilled over the well; today, there is no water; she hangs paper boats on branches in lieu of missing leaves. She carries a basket, its shape like an egg.

Birds curl against the woods' interior chanting *Birdcorpse, birdcorpse* between branches. A cat meows forcefully; all species communicate with difficulty. When she reaches the grocery store whose name she cannot remember, she chooses a carton of eggs. The cashier's apron is bright blue, unlike the sky, which is sky blue. The sea changes blue after it rains; blue thread strings across loose-leaf notebook paper.

Does the forest have an interior? She thinks and skips and pebbles graze across the stream. What conditions birds to plateau at certain heights? What causes a person to retreat from pleasure into numbness. There, 10,378 feet below the mountain's path—below the mountain's dirt, saltwater, and wooden footbridges—she feels a numb sensation. She thinks, *I feel nothing at all.*

Claire Donato

Wolf Bleeds to Death

by licking, again and again, the thin
flint blade flicked first with blood
from some other kill—elk or pig—
licking again and again until of the tongue
a mash is made, licking
still, again and again, slower
now, but still licking, fallen to its side
in the snow and staring at nothing
we can see.

Ross Gay

"Break In Case of Emergency"

Because her body had inspired both operas and border skirmishes involving machetes, it was decided she should be kept under glass. You've seen these glass boxes before—they hang on the walls in hidden, labyrinthine hallways in two-star hotels in almost-developing countries and have a sign on the front that says, "break only in case of emergency." And there is also usually a small metal stick, attached to the box by a silver chain, which can be used to break the glass. And with just the gentlest of strokes, the mildest of motions of the wrist, you can enjoy smashing something, and furthermore, because these boxes have been designed with the interests of the hotel staff in mind who have to clean up everything afterwards, all of the glass falls in a little heap at your feet. A lot of consideration for the working class has been taken into account in these matters. Which is to say, the slivers of glass, once shattered, however gently, should only require one flick of the broom. The things that go on in hotels, well . . . never mind about that. For now, anyway.

But that slender metal stick attached to the glass case was just too limpid for her. Because of her voluptuously incendiary nature, the diminuitive stick simply wasn't dramatic enough, and as there were, in her case, several emergencies a day [sometimes, twenty or thirty], you will not believe the implements that were wielded on behalf of springing her into the hallway, which was only the architectural prelude to a room, which was only the interior preface to a novel or an international incident, which often led to an accident on the balcony, or in Poland, involving vodka and a small revolver. Some bounded down the hallway with baseball bats; others came cartwheeling with samovar spouts, and others with those artisan knives you use for cutting foam boards and matte frames. But oh, those were practically nothing compared to the sticks of dynamite, molotov cocktails, crowbars, and long Russian poems that others used to break the glass.

You will wonder how it is that she could survive such breaking and entering, such ax-wielding cartwheeling, and when the Vikings were involved, such caterwauling [never mind the ravens that reeled overhead, like so many extras from a Hitchcock movie]. You might recall the late, dark night the Titanic went down? Well, it was like that, only the ice was on fire and you couldn't hang onto it. You see, there were many who sprung her from the glass case, but very few who could handle the contingent circumstances. Which is to say, it took a long time to bury all the bodies and the ambassadors never tired of making their requiems. It was finally decided that she should be moved to an undisclosed location, which is to say, to the libretto of an opera that was untranslatable. Sitting in row F, seat 19 of the opera house, you can hear, but not see her: she is lodged in the throat of the soprano who is trembling over her dead lover, yet also thinking of her next cigarette.

Eileen A. Joy

Most curious creature, Captain. The Sea Gull
has a tranquilizing effect on my sister
her body never touch her where
did they take her? They took her Where there's a seagull,
there's a whip I want to know what
killed these Tribbles. Fool me once
What am I?
a doctor, or a playwright? Ya fool me

I can't get fooled again, Chekhov
report: why did those Sea Gulls take my sister?
Captain: We're no strangers to love,
I know that human beings and sock puppets
can coexist peacefully, don't tell me
you're too blind to see? No
but I'd prefer not to, Jim, I'm a doctor
not an Argonaut— you wouldn't get this
from a couple of guys who were up to no good
started making trouble in Florida. They took my sister
and my mom got scared
she said: damnit, Will, I'm a seagull
not a doctor.

I'm a land surveyor, not a doctor. So where
did they take her? I want to know what
killed these tribbles are no strangers to love
the seagulls in Florida. yeah? go ahead. In Florida
we had hamburgers and there was a ship
quoth she. NO MORE HOME. So what am I
a doctor or a playwright? Chekhov: a word
was coming up on the screen; a couple of guys

I woke up this
morning with
and irrepressible
urge to play
Gauntlet II
and was of
course unable
having lost
my nintendo
long ago and
anyway there
was work to be
done for
example I
could do my
roomate's dishes or
apply to
anything
really as long
as that meant
coupling happiness
with an image
of progress
moving
linearly away
from memory
yet this god
damn game
when you
come to think

who were up to no good couldn't hold on
for over nine thousand years and she's
still not home. I was smashing pots, looking
for hearts when they took her, I turned
around and my mom got scared, she shouted
X-y-z-z-y but

I'm a land surveyor, not a doctor. So where
did they take her? I want to know what
killed these tribbles are no strangers to love
the seagulls in Florida. yeah? go ahead. In Florida
we had hamburgers and there was a ship
quoth she. NOMORE HOME. So what am I
a doctor or a playwright? Chekhov: a word
was coming up on the screen; a couple of guys

who were up to no good couldn't hold on
for over nine thousand years and she's
still not home. I was smashing pots, looking
for hearts when they took her, I turned
around and my mom got scared, she shouted
X-y-z-z-y but

Nothing happened. X-y-z-z-y Orpheus, don't play
that funky music it's dangerous
to go alone! When you swore you'd never TURN AR
OUND and desert me it's over my dead body
I've fallen and I can't get up; the nothing
happens. Down here, they say all your base are
belong to us, but there are no more base.
The seagulls hold me with their skinny hands

of it makes no
attempt to
explain itself
or motivate
players, except
starvation,
and the only
way to go is
deeper which
might be
enough for
people who
keep living
just for the
hell of it,
trusting
they'll get
theirs in the
end but the
game utilizes
a random level
generator,
which means
it goes on
forever—until
the player
dies, at least,
to look for a
reward outside
the labyrinth
misses the
point entirely;
as Althusser

34

Volta. Now this is a story all about how my life
got flipped, turned, and now, what rests
but that the mortal sentence stop at mere doubt.
From the cradle to the playground is where
you have let me down, you have turned, you
have got to be kidding me.

They look like good, strong hands
don't they know anything about art? e.g.
Thou art dead. No? We always thought
that's what it was: a sonnet, a heart container
a twisty maze of passages, all your base
are belong to seagulls took the top
of my head off while one who would pursue
commands us to awake, arise, x-y-z-z-y!

Nothing happens. It is only for the incomplete—
their tails cut off as they struggle with NOMORE
frostbit faces NOMORE beautiful than
a flowering meadow enriched with the hope
of redemption— for them alone we can say
well, at least that's over.

says, there is
no outside to
ideology You
play and play
and play and
then you die
or run out of
quarters if
you're at the
arcade though
home
entertainment
has largely
obscured the
role of
economics it
still seems like
I forgot something
and I can't
keep from
ending every
poem this way.

Chris Miller

Afterwords: Remy's Open Hand

What is this nonpower at the heart of power? What is its quality or modality? How should one take it into account? What right should be accorded it? To what extent does it concern us? Being able to suffer is no longer a power; it is a possibility without power, a possibility of the impossible. —**Derrida** [1]

Would that it had always been so, but by now, it should be a truism that the category "animal," this homogeneous mass of speechless, thoughtless, nonhuman lives unwittingly cloaked in Being, is metaphysical nonsense. Humans are animals too, no less unique in their habits and capacities than the others, and like them, as them, living through an ever shifting network of relations that itself renders the categories "individual" or "unity" as nonsensical as "animal" itself. Amid this flux, the human grasps after humanity, which is to say, its purportedly unique possession of reflective language, soul, reason, culture, and so on. And, thinking itself so uniquely capable, the human is what is not animal; above all, humans think themselves the life that can be murdered. Our ethical duty should be to recall animal suffering; recalling it, but no longer as contemptible weakness before human strength, our duty now should be to abandon the pride of our power and with it our unanimal humanity; having allowed ourselves to rejoin what we were all along, humans now will cease to imagine that only those creatures recognizably like humans—dolphins, great apes, pets, some (and only some) humans—belong to a rights-bearing community. Humans must now think and be thought by an ethics not of ability but of passivity, not of rights, but of being given over.

One past now, some 900 years ago, several monks discovered a wolf eating a deer in the forest, chased off the wolf, and took the carcass back with them to their monastery. But the wolf followed, and waited outside like a domesticated dog, until the abbot, Norbert of Xanten, realizing that no wolf would act so calmly without reason, compelled his monks to confess the injury they had done it. Norbert then ordered his monks to return what was not theirs, and the wolf, "finally taking [*accepta*] its prey," left in peace. Medieval Christianity allowed monks no more right to eat carrion sinlessly than it did anyone else: little could have driven these monks to this crime except their own desperation. Despite the monks' own need, despite the monks' humane generosity within this need to deliver the carcass over to their community, despite his own need, Norbert ruled against himself and his community. He decided to do justice, to let justice occur, though that justice meant he and his monks might starve. He gave back to the wolf—or the wolf, suffering no charity, took back what was his (for the Latin *accepta* means both "taking" and "receiving")—and, in so giving, in so having food snatched from his own hands, Norbert suspended his humanity, perhaps to the point of death.[2]

Another now, written roughly 1200 years ago, not so solemn: Saint Remy was accustomed to let sparrows eat grain out of his hand, an act that struck his companions, servants, and his biographer, Hincmar of Rheims, as undignified. Hincmar gilded Remy's generosity with interpretation: Remy, as if eluding the world's hostility due Adam and his descendants, dominated even wild animals; sparrows represent a host of virtues: their alacrity in avoiding traps teaches humans to avoid the devil. On the one hand, physical, on the other hand, hermeneutic containment, delivering animals again to human use. But somewhere in the midst of all this, Remy happily feeds the birds, a deed Hincmar finally remembers: for he finishes his memory by retelling an old story he found in Cassian's *Conferences*.

Once, when Cassian was gently stroking a partridge, a passing youth laughed to his friends: "Look how the old man plays with the bird just like a little boy!" But Cassian called over the boy, and asked him what he was carrying in his hand. "A bow," he said. Cassian, "And what's the use of what you're carrying in your other hand?" "They're arrows," he said, "for shooting beasts or birds or whatever else." Cassian asked, "And how do you use them?" The youth bent the bow, while Cassian watched and said nothing, waiting until the youth relaxed it. Cassian begged an explanation. The boy replied, "because the bow would be ruined if I bent it any longer." To which Cassian replied, "Likewise with the eagle, which can fly higher than any other birds, and gaze upon the sun, but which must descend from time to time; and likewise with us, here in this world of woe."[3]

This is a story about temporary abstinence from killing; about temporary abstinence from being human; but it is also, at its root, a story that demands hospitality, for in the *Conferences*, this is a story about community, about a hermit who occasionally entertains visitors, who sloughs off the scorn of his fellows with a parable about relaxation. Is Remy entertaining? Has he given himself up for the birds?

He has been hospitable. Derrida speaks of *hostipitalité*, holding together the double meaning of the French *hôte*: "guest" and "host." A host who welcomes a guest in a limited sense—for a limited time, with a limited set of accommodations, and for a guest whose character, desires, and needs are already known in advance—is no host at all, because any hospitality worthy of the name must be limitless. Thus the true host cannot welcome, because to welcome means to decide when and how far to open the door. A true host must risk being caught up entirely by the demands of the guest, even becoming hostage to the guest: hence the ethical and logical affinity of the opposing meanings of *hôte*. Hence too the presence of the Latin root *hostis*, meaning both "stranger" and "enemy."[4]

For what has Remy given? What has he given up? The swallows come; they eat to satiation while the saint's hand is open; in his passivity, the saint lets the swallows feed from him, heedless of their indifference to his sanctity. The true host, no longer human, among his animal guests, reserves to itself nothing, no capacity. This open hand, gradually emptied of food. Amid all this, this is all it is.

notes

[1] *The Animal That Therefore I Am*, ed. Marie-Louise Mallet, trans. David Wills (Fordham University Press, 2008), 28.

[2] *Vita Norberti*, ed. Roger Williams, in Georg Heinrich Pertz, *Historiae aevi Salici*, MGH SS 12 (Hanover: Impensis Bibliopolii Aulici Hahniani, 1856), 663-706, at 692.

[3] Loosely translated from *Vita Remigii Episcopi Remensis*, ed. Bruno Krusch in *Scriptores Rerum Merovingicarium* III, Monumenta Germaniae Historica (Hannover: Hahn, 1896), 239-341, at 266-68.

[4] "Hostipitality," in Jacques Derrida, *Acts of Religion*, ed. Gil Anidjar (New York: Routledge, 2002), 358-420.

Karl Steel

information,   submissions,   issues: http://
whiskeyandfox.org

**The other is indeed what is not inevitable, and it is there-
fore the only invention in the world, the only invention
of the world,** *our* **invention, the invention that invents** *us.*
Jacques Derrida